I Am a Human

A memoir on grief, identity, and hope

Pierce Taylor Hibbs

Other Books by the Author

The Trinity, Language, and Human Behavior

In Divine Company: Growing Closer to the God Who Speaks

Theological English: An Advanced ESL Text for Students of Theology

Finding God in the Ordinary

The Speaking Trinity & His Worded World

Struck Down but Not Destroyed: Living Faithfully with Anxiety

Still, Silent, and Strong: Meditations for the Anxious Heart, V. 1

Finding Hope in Hard Things: A Positive Take on Suffering

The Book of Giving: How the God Who Gives Can Make Us Givers

To receive free downloads and connect with the author, visit piercetaylorhibbs.com.

Copyright © 2022 Pierce Taylor Hibbs. All rights reserved. Except for brief quotations in critical publications or reviews, no part of this book may be reproduced in any manner without prior written permission from the author. For more information, visit piercetaylorhibbs.com.

Paperback ISBN: 978-1-7363411-8-6
Hardback ISBN: 978-1-7363411-9-3

Scripture quotations are from the ESV® Bible (The Holy Bible, English Standard Version®), copyright © 2001 by Crossway, a publishing ministry of Good News Publishers. Used by permission. All rights reserved.

For my dad, whose passing was a baptism. And for Christina, who has walked faithfully next to me in my grief.

Contents

Introduction   *1*

Transience   *3*

Limitation   *23*

Perspective   *47*

Hope   *59*

The Song of Being Human   *71*

Letter to Dad   *75*

"These are our few live seasons. Let us live them as purely as we can, in the present."

— Annie Dillard, *Pilgrim at Tinker Creek*

Introduction

I awoke this morning and had a conversation with the God of the universe. It was the rumble of the throat-clearing garbage truck that stirred me, following its meek headlights in the dark, the way a tired owner follows his dog.

"Thank you ... for the garbage collectors. They're up before all of us, clearing away the filth of the world, as you do." God responds with the silence that nods to truth. I pour my coffee and sit down on the couch, already drifting dazed on the soft current of time, the ever-running river.

Why can't we go back?
Why can't we forge ahead?
Why do we have to stay where we are?
Is there anything beyond it?

These questions, like apple skin, wrap tightly around me, housing the life-soaked and wondrous confusion underneath. And somewhere deep at the center, the apple seeds are sleeping in brown-black patience, comfortable in their own potential to make apple groves where we see grass.

What does it mean to be human? This is what I want to know. And how much meaning does one life have after it's gone?

Transience.
Limitation.
Perception.
Hope.

These are the four words I hold in my hands, the ones I was given in the morning dark. I'm going to set them free on the pages now. You watch with me. At the end, tell me if you know what it means to be human.

Transience

One of my earliest memories is dim but potent. It draws me to the depths of identity, need, behavior, shame, and sadness.

I was five. In the gold-orange twilight, I stood on the grassy hill in our back yard. We lived in a small, suburban neighborhood resting on the rolling landscape of eastern Pennsylvania. I'd asked my mom to make me a paper airplane. My dad wasn't home from work yet. She didn't know how, but she gave no indication. She pretended. She handed me a floppy, roughly folded sheet of paper and turned to go inside, walking quickly as I tossed the paper into the air, planning on flight. The paper rolled before me for a second and tumbled to the grass at my feet.

And then there was this moment, a Mona Lisa, this fraction of a second when I picked my head up and saw my mom rushing through the screen door with her head down. I felt something sink in the pith of my soul. I didn't know why. But I had never felt that way before, as if I were a robin about to jump into flight before realizing my plumage never came in, that I couldn't caress the wind with my feathered bones, the way I'd seen the other birds do.

Have you ever been grounded like that?

The world is a fragile place with so many birds robbed of flight. But we do fly eventually. And then we don't. And then we do.

* * *

Just before bed, I put down my book and picked up my journal.

> Are you ready to stop believing that you're immortal?" Not really. I've never been. It started when I remember breathing, and the sunset light pouring through the gold dust of summer, warming the brick on the house, painting the present with the aura of eternity. How could this ever come to an end? How could I part from the sound and the light? How could I leave when I only know how to arrive?

> We keep believing that we'll live forever, but it's a secret buried deep under the sediment of experience. Cancer can wash away that sediment, or Leukemia,

or a thousand other calls of death. But given enough time, the sediment settles again. The blinding truth of our transience is covered by tiny bits of rock . . . until it's dark. We can't stand in the light of our mortality very long. It starts to burn us. That's why we bury it. We bury the truth to avoid being burned by it; we cover over to carry on.

What if we didn't?

*   *   *

How much longer are you going to do this—drink a glass of water? Bite into bread? Push your muscles into the earth at a regular rhythm? Make love with your wife? How much longer?

And don't do that thing where you say, "Not forever," and then go back to forgetting about it, feigning eternity with regularity. You know better. You watched him die, remember? You watched him die in your living room.

But what else are you supposed to do? Treasure your moments like final drops of rain before a drought that never seems to come? Cry every time you bite into a sandwich? Write a sonnet for every step of your three-mile run? Of course not. Still, there's something here. What is it?

We're afraid of our transience. Ernest Becker said that we're always chasing heroism because we want to stand out and be remembered; we want to protest our death, to believe that somehow we'll live forever, and people will see us for the heroes we are.[1] There's some truth to this, but only some. Do you know why? Because all of it, in the end, is futile. We can't control how people perceive or remember us. We can't. But we're stubborn. We keep trying. At least, I do.

We want to believe that our transience is a bad dream, that we'll wake from it somehow, that we'll see our father didn't really disappear after the cancer. It was all a grand illusion. And then God opens his mouth: "What is your life? For you are a mist that appears for a little time and then vanishes" (James 4:14). That's transience. That's your life and mine: mist.

I still remember standing—eighteen years old—in a vacant hospital room just after learning that my father would die of cancer. I stared out the third-story window at the pipes that vented steam from mechanical systems on lower floors. The steam was

---

1. Ernest Becker, *The Denial of Death* (New York: Simon & Schuster, 1973), Part I: The Depth Psychology of Heroism, Kindle edition.

white and full-bodied and real . . . until it wasn't. It appeared only to disappear. Transparency came with elevation. That's me, isn't it?

I don't fully believe that I will die one day. Perhaps you don't either. Psychologists would say we have to constantly repress our fear of death in order to live. We disbelieve in our own death viscerally, even though we know conceptually that it's inevitable. That disbelief began to battle within me after I watched my father die. This book is a footnote to what I've learned about being human after the rock of that moment struck the glass surface of my young life.

But despite all I've learned and seen and experienced, part of me wishes I wasn't there that night in early June. (God, why did I have to be there? Why did I have to watch life trickle into silence like water slipping down into a cavern beneath the rock?) Something tells me I had to be there because the experience would be one of my greatest teachers. And here I am marking paper with my pen seventeen years later. It's still teaching—mostly the same lessons that I refuse to soak in.

What's it teaching? Transience. I have to keep writing that word just as you have to keep reading it. It's part of what it means to exist in this world. And yet it may be the part we most repress. I once heard in a movie that being young means secretly believing that you will be the one person who lives forever. But couldn't that also be a definition for being human? We know it's not true. The longer we live, the more acquainted we grow with exits. The subtle songs of life in persons go quiet. New songs cry into being. Everything overlaps. It's a symphony of going and coming, death and birth, silence and sound. We stand amidst the symphony in disbelief. Could our song really ever run quiet? Could it ever stop?

Two years after my father died, I had a mental and spiritual breakdown. I developed an anxiety disorder.[2] The world felt like one giant wet piece of paper, ripping into fuzzy seams all around me. Nothing held. I didn't understand death, and then I didn't understand life. I became a cripple in a functioning body. Even the simplest task required a spiritual cane. I couldn't hold myself up walking from the living room to the kitchen.

The truth of transience had pressed the air out of me. I was having to live in a new atmosphere all the sudden, with oxygen heavy as lead. I couldn't

---

2. I write about this in the context of my faith in *Struck Down but Not Destroyed: Living Faithfully with Anxiety* (Independently published, 2020).

get enough in. How could I find my footing if I was always moving? How does steam stand up?

* * *

In the early weeks and months of anxiety, I saw the whole world moving. They say the world spins 1,000 miles per hour. It's just so big that we can't feel it. But when you're shattered by anxiety, it's like you can feel it—the constant spinning. I was caught up in motion that was always faster than my feet. Leaves went through their color journey—the green of vigor, the yellow of maturity, the gold of fading glory, and the brown of bowing out. I used to gather them in my hands and crunch them into tiny pieces—little skeletons that once held sunlight. But then I was skeletal, a pressed and ossified memory of light. That was me now, wasn't it?

The 35-mph speed limit sign just down the street—bold, white, and shimmering in the summer—would gather dirt and rain residue as the days fell into autumn. In winter, it would darken even more with the shorter days, gray as the lonely clouds that loomed above. The summer-white glory was fading. That was me, wasn't it?

My clothes would be clean cotton, pressed and neat. And then the fabric would gather into tabs and let a forest of tiny threads stretch into the atmosphere. Eventually, my clothes would get donated to Good Will. That was me, wasn't it?

Transience. I was surrounded by it. I always had been, but I didn't notice until my father's respiratory system shut down in front of me, like an old train engine with no more coal in the furnace. Final breaths came counted.

Three. The exhalation was slow and settled.

Two. Wait. What's happening here? Life can't fully stop like this. We stared at his face as a collapsing star. Where does light go?

One. Hold on. Please.

And then the haunting realization that one soul had just been subtracted from the room. The star of his life had actually collapsed. His face rested like a stone on a riverbed. Decades of smiles and lifted cheeks, of furrowed brows and listening stares—all of it now behind closed doors of stillness.

Transience transforms us from one thing into another.

* * *

That night revealed one thing—and it kept revealing it through the years: we cannot stop the movement. The river will run. The leaves will turn. The flowers will fade. The sun will rise. What's new is always standing on the broad shoulders of what's old. Things. Keep. Changing. You know this. They put it in Hallmark cards.

I hated it then, and sometimes I still hate it. So much is lost, isn't it? It's like the whole world is dammed by a barricade too low and too weak. Everything is pouring over the top and falling down to an unsearchable bottom. And we're running around with buckets trying to scoop something up—anything—to save it. But our buckets are bottomless.

Still, that doesn't keep us from trying to fill them, to hold on to what's already over the edge of the cliff. Why do you think we value pictures so much? They're attempts to capture what's just about to pass over the lip of the dam.

God help us. What are we doing? Fighting with transience. Fighting with time.

* * *

This is the darker side of transience. But there is a brighter side, too. Doesn't there have to be?

Transience can be a river running over a cliff edge, where we slap the water and rage against loss. But it can also be a song. And songs would be nothing without beginnings and endings.

* * *

My father was a song. The first notes struck the world in October of 1955. First-born baby boy—dark hair, dark eyebrows, dark eyes, with a frown mirroring his mother's. Then those first months of being carried through the living room and kitchen like a gold feather... light, precious, fragile, and worthy of arms. Open eyes like doors to every color—the blue carpet, the tan linoleum floor, the gray-brown bark of the one tree in the front yard.

And sounds: vibrations from his mother's vocal chords calming his settled breaths; the robins and cardinals singing their God-given refrains as they danced around the garden, with its monstrous, red tomatoes; the occasional swish of a car calling out movement in the wider world.

The next notes came married to the previous ones—the bold notes of toddlerhood, when his feet found their footing on that blue carpet, on the patchwork of grass and tree roots on the front lawn, on the cement sidewalk with its commanding straight lines. Day after day in a world of giants and trees that disappeared into the sky. And the sunlight on the walls, painting branches that seemed to wave in water, the shadow and the light . . . the dancing.

His song changed with the strange and painful entrance of otherness: brother first, then sister. He was not the only one. New songs played alongside his own, bringing that classic frown to the foreground. Light and color and sound—by that point—had moved from "wild" to "world."

A string of high notes comes with the thrill of jumping, of running, of falling. The world has hard edges. Gravity doesn't compromise. His knees have taught him this.

How the song of boyhood must have seemed eternal, the sounds and smells and sights—vibrant and ageless. The familiar rhythm of the train that brought their father to and from work, with its defiant horn announcing his steel-tracked presence.

But the eternality of boyhood fades, sometimes sharply with shame, but mostly with softness, in little movements of independence: opening the fridge door, walking to the basement without the handrails, getting hit with a baseball in the thigh.

The song keeps playing as his breath holds the baseline, readying his body for movement and his mind for thoughts. Some are little: Why does his mother play the piano? Others are Everest-like: Who is God? Is he behind the sun? How did I get here?

Oh, the song, bound to his name: Donald Ray Hibbs. The song through awkward, big-clothed adolescence and trim-fitting teens, the song that was his identity, the song that played without his effort or attention.

How the melody deepened when he held his firstborn, the child turned father. And the song through his fatherly years, woven with black hair, hammer swings, and raw, split wood. His deep and weathered voice, booming from the pulpit in passion and praise for Jesus Christ and the beautifully true dream of redemption, a hope warring through and behind all he could see.

How the song turned quiet in the days when his sons had to turn his body in the hospital bed—all those fine black hairs dusting the white pillow case and bedding. The song moving toward silence on that warm June evening.

What a song . . . to drop your jaw and draw out your tears with its richly colored, sound-swollen beauty.

* * *

Transience is the song of every life. And you can't get angry at songs for having a beginning and an end. That is what makes them.

Of course, I want to hear his song again, to soak in every sound, every second, every grin and grimace, every handshake and hammer swing. But what makes the song so beautiful is the simple truth that it only plays once.

* * *

Here I am at my kitchen table, made of old barn wood that I sanded down in the chill of October, because my father taught me how. His life and time have been poured into me. I carry his blood, his memory, as I live out my own song, which started while his was still playing. The harmony of life, generation to generation, carries the sound forward. Here I sing, with his hand-me-down notes. I am part of him as he is part of me. His transience is now my transience. His fading became my flourishing, just as my fading will be my son's and daughters' flourishing. Transience is not just one song; it's many songs woven together.

* * *

Dad, do you see me? I'm still at the kitchen table, pinning my thoughts to paper, trying to make a map of the past for my future. Am I getting the lines right? Will anyone be able to follow this?

What do I do with transience, with song, with my metered days? Three paths, I think: grief, greed, and gratitude. I've taken each in turn, haven't I?

Grief: the dull throb of wanting the lost. Greed: the insatiable appetite for things that don't last, a grand plan of self-centered distraction. Gratitude: seeing a million gifts in a million places. Your father was one of them. He was given. Just like your mother, your brothers, your bones, skin, and breath. You woke up to abundant Christmas morning. Will you really choose sorrow and anger over joy and worship? Find the one who gave all this to you. And spend the rest of your days staring at him.

* * *

Transience is part of what it means to be a human, to be mist, to be one winter morning, one season, one flower fading, bound to bow back to the ground. God, I spend most of my moments trying to ignore transience, and the rest sulking at its seniority. Transience will always rule over me . . . except in one way. I almost can't wait to say it. But I will wait.

* * *

Oh, never mind. I'm terrible at waiting. You always knew that, dad, didn't you?

The poet Christian Wiman wrote that "Christ is contingency."[3] What he meant was that believing in Christ is believing in and through uncertainty—not to treat faith as a rock that destroys anything in its path but as a current constantly carrying us to

---

3. Christian Wiman, *My Bright Abyss: Meditation of a Modern Believer* (New York: Farrar, Straus and Giroux, 2013), 16.

new places. Jesus Christ, the two-thousand-year-old dead and raised Nazarene, is with us in that current, through the white rapids that throw us into the air, through the bends and sways of our bodies. Christ is there in the change, not despite it.

This is another way of saying that God himself—how could this be?—is present in our transience. And if that's true, then transience isn't accidental. It's not an uncontrollable decay or a disease that spreads, something we have to vaccinate ourselves against. Transience is a means of travel.

* * *

I think on this at the kitchen table, still mourning the death of my father seventeen years later. Why? If I mourn his leaving, then I mourn my own. If I weep for his transience, then I weep for mine. True—I miss him fiercely. God, how I wish he could just show up for a second to say, "I'm proud of you. Keep walking." All these years I've mourned his passing, his transience, because I want to take something back. I want to hear his song again. I want transience to go on coffee break.

But the longer I mourn that, the more deeply I will mourn my own life, that I am a season, a song, one glorious dawn.

You want hope? Here it is: Transience happens with eternity in your midst. The God of seasons, of song, the maker of moments, is in your chest. The marvel of life, even of the loss of it, is continuance beyond conclusion. Transience is preparing us for the next great change. It's not stealing from us. God owns time, and no one can steal from him. Transience is a teacher. The lessons sting. They make us weep—as I did in that church so many years ago, with my father's casket resting on the carpet like a stick on the stones. But that day was one, in a month, in a season, in a year, in a decade. You get the idea: Transience doesn't just mean ending; it means continuing; it means traveling.

* * *

Who I am right now is not who I was then—with my fears and dreams and insecurities. Nor is it who I will be tomorrow, or in five minutes. Transience is always teaching. The God of eternity entered into transience for us, with us, through us. We can't see him, which is a beauty in itself. For if we saw him, he would change. That's what the visible world does.

The eternal must be invisible . . . for now. Transience cannot touch the inward parts of God, as time cannot touch the inner parts of eternity. And so we won't see God on the river of time with us. But that's because he's buried himself in our being, in our becoming. Transience carries us forward. Time shapes us. Age alters us. But everything is not lost. In fact, nothing that matters is ever lost. Not me. Not my father. Transience is in the hands of eternity, the hands of a God with perfect and incalculable memory. God knows every note in my father's song, every knee scrape and hair follicle and daydream. What transience seemed to take is forever in God's pockets.

* * *

Do you see the hope? What does it mean to be a human? It means living in transience—as the mist, the season, the wildflower—with eternity in your chest.

I will have to keep learning this. Maybe every day. I'm still confused. I still grasp at things—feelings, ambitions, joys, persons—as if transience could be overcome, as if I could vaccinate myself against it or at least pretend it wasn't running beneath me as a river all the time. I want my father back.

But I know now that to say this would be to ask for his transience to be reversed, for his change to be revoked, for his eternity to return to time. And that would be a terrible thing. I don't want my dad back here. I want to be where and when he is. And I will be. I will be . . . when transience finishes my song.

* * *

If being a human means being in transience, then what am I to do?

Bind myself to the present. Weep with those who weep. Rejoice with those who rejoice. Drink a glass of water. Bite into bread (good bread). Feel your feet touch the carpet. Make love with your wife. Laugh with wildness when your daughter comes up with a new dance to the melody of "I Want a Hippopatamus for Christmas." Bind yourself to the present.

But know that, in faith, you're married to eternity. God is in your chest.

Limitation

Limitation is a son of transience. When things are always changing, when waves of time are always lapping at the thin shore of the present, we see how little we're able to control. We hate this instinctively. And then we draw the false conclusion that limitation is an evil, that we have to wage against it until our minds crack or our bodies crumble.

But limitation is the very thing that opens us to relationship. A limitless being needs no relationships. God didn't need a relationship with us; he wanted one. I'll never understand why, and I don't need to. The important thing is that, for us, limitation is built into our being for divine reasons. Limitation is a relay race. It shows us how far we can go before we need to hand the baton off to someone else, or receive it from another runner.

The dark side of this is death. As my father lay dying in our living room, a feeding tube winding its way from his black-haired stomach, his limitation was painfully foregrounded. It screamed at us, every time we had to pour a cup of Nutri-fast into the gastronomy tube. We had to put the food right into his stomach. His mouth was a dry cave leading to a dark and vacant road. We cheated him. His limitation at this stage was sickening.

But that sickening limitation opened a place for us to care for him in his final days, as did his limitation for managing pain, when morphine entered his clenched teeth, through a mouth I had to pry open with all my teenage might.

Other limitations are less severe, but they do the same thing: create spaces for relationships. Relationships can only enter when need or desire provides the space, but need and desire are both peninsulas. They call out for ships. They need ports filled and decks unloaded. Every need and desire is a shipyard. We're always searching for sails. That's limitation.

The afternoon we learned that my father's brain cancer was beyond treatment, my mother and I drove through the car-cluttered parking lot for an eternity. "I just don't know how to live my life without him in it," she said with tears. I held it together until, by providence, we came to a big red sign that said, "Stop." Stop, Taylor. Just. Stop.

So I did. I cried at the stop sign. I cried because he had to stop. I cried because of his limitation, and my limitation, and my mom's limitation. We were at the great impasse, the wall between life and death that draws out weeping from us on one side and silence from those on the other.

Limitation is rarely painless. But that's because we have an ingrained desire to be self-sufficient. And that desire is never going to be met. Never. That might sound horrible, but think of it this way: Limitation will show you what you can really give.

The poet I referenced earlier, Christian Wiman, struggling with an uncurable terminal illness, wrote,

> In truth, experience means nothing if it does not mean beyond itself: we mean nothing unless and until our hard-won meanings are internalized and catalyzed within the lives of others. There is something I am meant to see, something for which my own situation and suffering are the lens, but the cost of such seeing . . . may very well be any final clarity or perspective on my own life, my own faith. That would not be a bad fate, to burn up like the booster engine that falls away from the

throttling rocket, lighting a little dark as I go.[1]

My father was a booster engine. For me. For my brothers. For my mother. For hundreds of others with the words and memories he left behind as he blasted into the star-singing dark. We're all destined to be booster engines.

* * *

Limitation, I said, is not an evil. It's only an evil in a world full of people striving for autonomy. To be limited is to be made for relationship, to be made as a puzzle piece with edges and curves searching for correspondence, for extension. Loss just makes this obvious.

But there is a want—no, a need so deep and so broad that nothing here can satisfy it. It's the edge of our puzzle piece that can't seem to find a perfect match. We get close sometimes, try to force a fit, but in the end we'll admit we never really had it. And that's because, despite all our comforts and loves in life, we know we're foreigners on planet earth, don't

---

1. Christian Wiman, *My Bright Abyss: Meditation of a Modern Believer* (New York: Farrar, Straus and Giroux, 2013), 162.

we? Search yourself. There is something deep in the caverns of every soul, a whistling other worldly melody. Maybe death is what opens our ears to it.

On a sunny, cloudless May afternoon, I walked down the tiled hallway to my father's hospital room. We had made the decision to bring him home for hospice care. And we told him he was coming home. We kept using that word, "home," as if we actually knew what it meant.

As I walked through the doorway, the man I knew as strength itself was covered in thin sheets and sunlight, staring out the five-foot window at the sky. Tubes and wires ran their way from his body to gray machines that spoke a simple language of lights and numbers. A man of sheets and wires—this is what it had come to.

"You know we're bringing you home, right?" I said. "You know why we're bringing you home?"

He turned and raised his thin, left arm into the air, pointing into the blue expanse like some kind of tired captain. And he managed to get out just one word: "home."

Death teaches us that we're foreigners here, exiles. All of our limitations culminate in the most terrifying limitation: our limited breath. Home cannot be found here. It is in another country, continents away, beyond the ocean of familiarity. As the wise mole said in Charlie Mackesy's brilliant little book: "I think everyone is just trying to get home."[2]

We enjoy our temporary stand-ins for home. As I write these words, I sit at the kitchen table that's held a thousand meals before me. My back knows this chair. My elbows know the proud-grained oak surface. My fingers caress the grain and the barren nail holes of the old barn wood I've sanded down. This is my home. But I know I can't stay here forever. And that limitation makes me a foreigner, an exile.

But as Eugene Peterson wrote, "Exile is the worst that reveals the best."[3] If I'm not fully home here, then I will be fully home elsewhere. My father knew that as he pointed into the blue sky on that May afternoon.

The limit of life makes foreigners of us all.

* * *

If the limit of life makes us foreigners, why do

---

2. Charlie Mackesy, *The Boy, the Mole, the Fox, and the Horse* (New York: HarperOne, 2019).

3. Eugene H. Peterson, *Run with the Horses: The Quest for Life at Its Best*, Commemorative ed. (Downers Grove, IL: IVP, 2019), 152.

we spend such little effort daydreaming about our eternal home? Disbelief. Lean on that word for a moment.

Disbelief. Just as we disbelieve our transience, we disbelieve our limitation. But we also disbelieve in an eternal home. Surely, we must be able to live here forever. Surely, we can push past the limits of life and somehow, someway keep existing here. Surely this place can be made a home.

And so we go hunting for the comfort and security of home in a place that cannot be our home. C.S. Lewis wrote, "If I find in myself desires which nothing in this world can satisfy, then the most logical explanation is that I was made for another world."

Another world—a world without death, a true home, a place we can stay. There is a country to which we are native, and it is not here.

* * *

Getting to our home country means accepting the limitation of death, as my father did, pointing out that hospital window at the blue expanse.

The Apostle Paul wrote, "What you sow does not

come to life unless it dies" (1 Cor. 15:36). Death is the great limitation we all face. But life—home—is on the other side of it. We have to go through the clouds to get to the blue sky.

My problem has been death-denial. I've had a sort of PTSD response to watching my father die in front of me. Death has been a terror, a black beast in the shadows calling my name. I used to never think of death, or I'd flee from the thought whenever it came. I saw death as a devil, a harrowing limitation to all I knew and loved.

But if Paul is right, then death is not a devil; it's a door. It's how we get home. It's how we stop being foreigners. It's where we leave the pilgrimage behind.

* * *

As a kid, I was scared of waterslides. Our parents took us to a water park for the day when I was around eight or nine. I remember the shining, light blue plastic of the halfpipes, the sound of rushing water, my dad's body covered in thick, black hair. I stood at the top staring at the streaming water. My dad went first to show me it was okay. I watched his body slide away, and then it was my turn. I gripped the hard edges of the half-pipe, pushed off and laid back on the hard plastic. As I moved, I trusted. "Dad went first. It's okay."

God does this for us. Did you know that? I didn't.

God has a Son, a child who is one with him. He was born two thousand years ago in a tiny village. His feet padded the dirt and the grass. His tastebuds knew what salt was. His eyes had to adjust to the morning light. He could bend his fingers and toes. He could hear sounds and feel the heart of a hearth on his skin. He had a body, just like mine. He was a pilgrim, too. He could feel in his fingertips the sense of travel, of continuous movement from one day into the next, never feeling truly at home. He was a traveler. He was a kernel of wheat. Once he even said, "Unless a grain of wheat falls into the earth and dies, it remains alone; but if it dies, it bears much fruit" (John 12:24). Fruit. New life. Growth in color—these things follow death?

Keep in mind that this is God talking. God is saying these things. God is saying that life follows death.

But he didn't just say it. God let himself hang from a tree, killed by hands and muscles of those he loved. The life that he made took life from him. And he let himself hang there like a ready seed, set to fall into the earth, and then to grow, to climb from the dark with color and scent and breath. From the kernel of his earthly life came fruit imperishable. He went first, knowing every single human would be staring at him, trying to see if it was safe, just as I did at the top of that waterslide so many years ago. God went first. He showed us that death is a door. My father believed this. He went home that May in 2004 with a belief that his pilgrimage was ending. Home was on the horizon. Home. And his wild God cut the trail for him, straight through the dense thicket of doubt.

Death is the limitation that leads to preservation, the ancient terror that leads to new trees, the shadow before the sun.

* * *

Death as limitation is also the white brush that paints everything lighter. All that seems eternally stable, strong as granite, takes on a lighter hue when we think of death.

In one of the earlier weeks in April of 2004, when my father could still speak, he asked us to take him for a drive. "Why?" we asked. "They need a car," he said.

He was talking about me and my older brother. He knew that he was dying and wanted me and Trevorr to have a car we could use to get to and from work. Along the strip by the Lehigh Valley Hospital there were mostly high-end dealers: Mercedes, BMW, Jaguar. For a family that lived not too high above the poverty line, this was laughable. It's embarrassing enough to drive an old Plymouth minivan onto a lot full of Jaguars, but even worse when you try to believe that maybe you could belong there. "We can't look for cars here," my mom said. "These are sports cars."

My dad nodded reluctantly, and so we turned the car around and went back to the hospital parking lot where we belonged. Even now, in my memory, those Jaguars are shrouded in a white haze. My father's impending death turned those cars into feathers. In the face of death, they might as well have blown away in a breeze.

The strange thing about growing up without much money is that you start to dream about having some one day, as if it mattered, as if it could solve problems. But money is really just good for helping people pretend that death is a fiction. You realize this eventually, even if it takes decades, and then you're back where you started: thinking that you might as well have no money if it's just going to get in the way of the truth.

I still deal with this now, even though I know better. I think, "If I just had a little more money, I could solve some problems, fret less about finances." But people who drive Jaguars still die—of cancer, heart failure, kidney failure, head trauma. Death still takes everything. It paints the whole world in white, making the hard and deep colors of material things somehow lighter. Jaguars covered in snow. Mansions draped in dust. Everything gets white-washed.

*   *   *

Limits also struck my father's tongue, not long after that drive to high-end car dealerships. Revoked speech was a painful limitation, a turning away from consonants and vowels, the empty streets of syllables, a ghost-town of expression filled only with silence and watching eyes. The pressure put on his brain stem had removed nearly all ability to speak. Conversations were had for him, not with him. If friends came to visit, he would be the animated portrait, expressing his thoughts through cheek muscles and eyebrows.

The absence of speech came not long before the "Dutch crumb incident." Conversations in those final weeks petered out into puddles—shallow topics that might draw out a few smiles. Two of his friends began to talk about their favorite donuts. When they asked my dad, the only word he managed to get out was, "Europe." Then came the guessing, for some thirty minutes. German chocolate. French cruller. Did Russia have a donut?

We didn't figure it out while I was there, but I later found out the answer: Dutch crumb. A small donut shop that he'd frequented over the years made a heavy cake donut covered in glaze, sugar, and crumbs (basically just more sugar). That was his donut. Years later I would buy Dutch crumb donuts from the same shop and give them to my students. "Language is a gift," I would say. It is given, and it is taken.

* * *

I will keep the refrain going: Limitations always allow for relationships. When he lost his speech, we spoke for him. When he lost his movement, we moved his body. When he lost his life, we carried that body, first to the church, then to the cemetery. Limitations leave us open for others.

We think of limitations as barriers, as obstacles. But all the way back at the eye-slit dawn of creation, we were made with limitations. How else would we be able to relate to the life-Spirit that breathed himself into us? Limitations are harbors for love. Our limitations are the very things that direct our gaze towards others, towards God, who has conquered the greatest limitation: death itself. We stare at God because we're limited. We stare at others because we're limited. Limitation means we're always looking for exchange and interaction. As the poet David Whyte wrote, "We are made for unending meeting and exchange."[4] But being made for that also means being made with limitations. We're taught so much to be independent that we forget it's a fiction. No one is independent, except for God, and he chose to engage with others. What does that tell you about independence? It's overrated, and it's a ridiculous aspiration. Sooner or later, you are going to rely heavily on others for your daily existence. In fact, you already do. Was my father any less reliant on others

---

4. David Whyte, *Consolations: The Solace, Nourishment, and Underlying Meaning of Everyday Words* (Langley, WA: Many Rivers, 2018), 221.

when he could speak? Yes in one sense; no in another. Even those who speak would be mute with no one to speak to. We're always relying on others. Death just makes it blatant by burning up any daydreams of bravado.

What are we after? What do we want? To think well of ourselves? Why? We're good at answering questions no one asks, and embarrassingly bad at asking questions we need answered.

"Who are you?" asked the caterpillar from Alice in Wonderland. She could have said, "I'm transient and limited. Who are you?" The caterpillar would have said the same, and they could have had a nice discussion on their existential dilemma. As it happened, they both tried to claim an identity in feigned isolation from others. And we do, too.

We're scared of being limited because we don't want to admit that we need help. We always need help. Always. Even on our best days, when we're cruising down the freeway in a Jaguar and munching on a Dutch crumb donut. We just get dangerously good at pretending we don't need help. One of the beautiful lines from Mackesy's book comes from the mouth of a horse. "'What is the bravest thing you've ever said?' asked the boy. 'Help,' said the horse."[5] We seem to think help is a resignation when it's actually an extension.

* * *

My three- and six-year-old are counting out change on the coffee table. They never met my father. They've just heard stories. They know of his limitations, his death. And they know that made Daddy very sad. But right now they're trying to count to ten and build a "royal money store." I don't know what that is. I'm limited, just as they are. We don't grow out of limitation; we just grow into it.

The girls have now moved the royal money store to the three-year-old's fist. Everything is accounted for. They'll find a safer place soon enough, one that doesn't sweat on the coins. Or maybe they'll abandon the coins altogether. The coins hold as much value to them as broken crayons. They don't need them anymore.

A day came when my father would say that of his own arms and legs. What good is a breaking body when a caged spirit is begging for flight?

---

5. Mackesy, *The Boy, the Mole, the Fox, and the Horse.*

Limitation helps us play. But it also helps us fly. And we will all fly one day.

* * *

Eugene Peterson wrote, "No life is complete until there's a death. Death sets limits. To be human is to die. By dying, we attest to our humanity. Death doesn't so much terminate our humanity as prove it."[6]

At eighteen years old, I didn't know this. And even if I had, it wouldn't have helped much. Knowing death as limitation does little for the living who know death as absence. Unless we're talking about our own death. And I wasn't thinking of my own death when my father died. That would come later.

My father's limitation, his death, was searing. It tore something out of me, as if the root bulb of his life were entangled with my own. Dirt was lost as his tendrils were ripped from mine. The limitation of death is painful for the living.

But not only painful. His death cracked the eggshell around my soul. Inside was a super-

---

6. Eugene H. Peterson, *Leap over a Wall: Earthy Spirituality for Everyday Christians* (San Francisco: HarperOne, 1998), 217.

sensitive creature—feeling too much, seeing too much, hearing too much, tasting too much. I had been protected from living an overwhelmed life. But that also meant I was protected from depth, from a potent, otherworldly passion, from a real and sincere faith that reached beyond myself.

Peterson goes on to write, "If we don't give our full attention to death, but spend our lives avoiding the subject and obscuring it with euphemisms, we diminish our lives. Denial of death is avoidance of life."[7] Before my father's limited life, I had lived diminished, and I didn't even know it. I was ignorant experientially of the passion and praise other tortured souls offered up on pages. John Keats. Samuel Taylor Coleridge. Henry David Thoreau. These were voices crying from mountain tops. I loved to listen to them . . . but I neglected the plain truth that to really "get" them, I would need to climb a mountain, adjust to the thin air, stare into the navy sky, focus on the distant stars, wait for movement.

My father's death broke the eggshell around my soul and demanded a march, a travel. That's what the deaths of others do to us: they make us travelers. Up the mountain I would go . . . with anxiety, with labored

---

7. Peterson, *Leap over a Wall*, 218.

breaths, with a raw heart. Up the mountain into the thin, clear air of grief, where the topography below seems flat and the expanse above is frustratingly eternal. Up the mountain I went.

*   *   *

Having been up to the peak of that mountain, I can tell you that nothing much happens at the top. You get lonely with your reveries. Memories drift in and out of your line of vision. But you're different when you come back down. Maybe a part of you stays up there. Things are the same when you get back to the valley. But you see more of the world around you, paint every moment with questions.

I just went outside to stack firewood on the first of the year. I wanted to feel the wood grain on my skin, wanted my fingers to chill. I rubbed the decayed bark in my fingers. This is the stuff my body will lay in one day? This?

I remind myself of my favorite words from Henry Wadsworth Longfellow:

> Life is real, life is earnest,
> And the grave is not its goal.

'Dust thou art, to dust returneth'
Was not spoken of the soul.

I am more. My father was more. Souls don't go down; they go up. They go home.

I have given my full attention to death, Eugene. All of it. My father was limited. I am limited. But there is someone unlimited, with an unlimited home, unlimited time, unlimited love. I am limited and bound for the unlimited.

On the other side of the mountain of grief, I have found there is more than our limitations.

Limitation sets us up for relationships, but it also sets us up for faith. Faith takes us beyond the limits of the familiar, toward the horizon, too far ahead to fathom.

Without limitation, we would be trapped. We'd be less human, not more. Why? I believe we are made for faith, made to offer a response of trust to what we cannot understand. Trust. And the limitations of ourselves and others provide occasions for faith and trust.

> Every life is a limitation on my life. Those closest to me limit me most. Children are a

limitation; spouses are a limitation; parents are a limitation. These limitations aren't minor inconveniences; they're major and unavoidable conditions in the all-demanding exercise of being human. Given our propensity for wanting to live not as humans but as gods and goddesses, it's quite inevitable that from time to time we fantasize an end to the limitations: death of the other as freedom of the sovereign self.

But it never works out that way; honoring the limits, giving dignity to the death, is what deepens life. Those who take a firm and prayerful stand against the removal of limits know what they're doing: ridding ourselves of inconvenient lives that seem to interfere with our living results not in more life for us, but less.[8]

My father's death led to more life, not less. His life was the grain of wheat that fell from the stalk stretching in the sun. My life will be that for my kids one day. Wheat is meant to fall in a fallen world. When it does, growth happens.

---

8. Peterson, *Leap over a Wall*, 221–222.

Growth happens in the earth, where it's dark and damp, where sunlight doesn't reach. Growth in faith happens when you need light, not when you have it.

* * *

Transience. Limitation. To us, they are dark brushstrokes on the canvas of time. I still struggle with my father's death. I try to beat transience by writing books that will outlast me, by ignoring my own death, by pretending eternity is within time. I still get tight-throated when we drive past Lehigh Valley Hospital, where we received news that he wouldn't "make it" (what does it mean to "make it," really?). I hate transience most of the time. It tastes bitter.

And limitation runs a similar course. I try to ignore it, evade it, take other paths in the woods of my mind, move around its hedges. But it stays. Just as transience stays.

One of the great lessons God continues to teach me is that transience and limitation are not accidents in a world spinning in the dark. The all-consuming, ever-whispering life-Spirit of God reins them as horses, directing and guiding, never for a millisecond losing control. Transience and limitation don't destroy us;

they define us. And they refine us. They open our eyes to the beauty and wonder—and, yes, terror—of being alive in this pulsing, breathing, colored world. What did I do to get here, to accept life, to move my fingers, to have cartilage in my knees ossify into kneecaps? Nothing. All is gift.

The meaning and identity we find amidst grief—what I'm still finding as I mourn my father and long for resurrection and unending life with this Spirit inside me, this animating energy of me—result from seeing ourselves truly in this world.

I am a mist. I don't feel like one most of the time, but I am. I am limited. I don't want to be most of the time, but I am.

The real question is this: what am I going to do here? What am I going to do right now? Make. Speak. Move. Touch. Pray. Read. Smile. Fight. Weep. All these and more.

But I'm going to do everything from a certain place. For me, it's a place of hope, of joy and gratitude that wars against doubt and despair, of faith that things are more than they appear to be. They are more.

Dad, I miss you. I want to see you and touch your sandpaper face again, to embrace your body (several inches shorter than my own). But if you hadn't died,

I would never be chasing after the more, the deeper beauty behind life's fragility, the God who thunders and whispers and works with shadows and light. I am after the more.

Perspective

From a certain place—that's me. My place. My place is my uniqueness. What I see from here, and what I have seen, that is who I am. No one else in the universe, in history, has my place. Many have lost fathers, but not my father. Many have embraced brothers, but not my brothers. We are the place that God has given us. Not only this, but always this.

* * *

I have seen the long, winding road through the trees that ends at a white church resting on the collar bone of a pond. I have seen the deep red fabric of the upholstered pews, soaking in the speech of God that bounded forth from the golden oak pulpit. My father stood there when I was a boy, though I remember the pea-sized gravel stones in the parking lot more than what he actually said, the view of congregant shoes from beneath the pews more than the life-and-death words falling into the thick air.

I have seen the blood on my father's neck after a fresh shave, red streams among a thousand truncated trees.

I have seen the orange flame of our wood stove flicker and fade, in its cast-iron home, hugging the wood my dad had split and stacked in the musty garage—the light consuming it, turning the pith into heat and smoke.

I have seen red hair after red hair push through my Irish beard, filling in through the years, day by silent day. Dad, I look like you.

Yesterday evening my daughter saw blood on my neck from shaving. The horror in her eyes (why wasn't I crying for a Band-Aid?)—I saw it. I've come full circle. Now I am the man with sandpaper skin, whose chin has been touched by smaller hands.

* * *

I am transient. I am limited. I am here, in this place. What I've seen I carry with me, like old books in a satchel, and what I carry shapes what I see. This is the ring of perspective, the arc of the past bending into the arc of the present bending into the arc of the future. No person's arcs perfectly match those of another. The arcs we hold set us in our own boat at the harbor of each day. Right now—now—I'm in the water, in a place of my own. I write to tell you where I am.

* * *

Dad, you had your boat. Cancer diagnosis at thirty-five. Rough water after, the speck of your vessel lifting and lowering on waves well beyond you. What did you do?

You believed.

* * *

That continuous decision—to believe—is what you gave to me, your message in a glass bottle that bumped into the hull of my own boat. "Believe."

You were a God-chaser, as I am now, scanning the horizon for divine scents, colors, whispers. And then it's to the oars.

* * *

I watched you: back bent over the table, staring

into a black book—the speech of God—while transient steam from coffee disappeared just above your head. You God-chaser, running on words that opened doors inside you. I know the feeling now. I run on top of your words, from a new place. My feet are always standing on your back. I see more because you have laid down to rest.

* * *

Sometimes I want a different boat, a different vantage point, on calmer waters. But what can I do? Jump ship? It's just me on the water here, with my quiet God. This is my boat. I am here, with my hurt, with my memory, with my marvel and desire. I am here, at the kitchen table again before dawn. I am my ever-moving place, with a thousand memory fragments tattooed on my face with invisible ink. I see from what I've seen.

* * *

I was timid. I was shy. Do you remember that gold afternoon in the early 90s, when I stepped out of the van as a six-year-old, onto a field crawling with other kids kicking soccer balls? It felt like they were in a moment far from me. I couldn't go there, could I?

You asked me to try, to row the boat of my quiet life next to their churning legs and flopping hair. To go there? I still remember the terror, the desire to turn back.

But I tried. I tried. And then, miraculously, I saw that all of them were in boats, too, bobbing on the present, letting go of all except that dusted ball. I liked this. I learned to love it. My feet—they stomped the grass and dirt in abandoned worship. Life was the chase, the kick, the net.

Shyness is a fence, not a wall. You guided me to a gate. Thank you.

* * *

That moment on the hazy soccer fields in 1991 makes me think of "Blackbird" by the Beatles. I remember hearing my father play it. He was a musician, as well as a preacher and a carpenter.

Blackbird fly.
Blackbird fly.
Into the light of a dark black night.

Isn't that what growth is like? Lifting your feeble wings and letting go of the perch of the past for the openness of the present? I was a blackbird that day. I am a blackbird right now. We're always clutching branches beneath us when the wild God of the unknown is beckoning us into the air.

* * *

My place, my perspective, is unique. It is the only one of its kind. I feel it in my knee as it's pressed up against the bottom of the oak boards at our kitchen table. I feel it in my bones as my fingers press and push this copper pen. To be yourself is to be where you are and to see all from that place. It is to know, in the moment, the fears, hopes, and memories that shape your vision. My identity is perspectival. I see from this place.

And this place is swollen with the fears and hopes that have emerged like light from the eye-slit crack in the shelled soul of me, a crack set in that shell by my father's death. And now I act, I feel, I think in that light, from this place of losing and finding.

* * *

My fears and hopes and actions from this place are still tainted by pain, stained like a white napkin under a used teabag.

My wife always pulls me into myself. On the highway, amidst the narration of an audiobook for our kids, we realized some disturbing truths.

I write so incessantly because I'm afraid of dying too young, like my father. Seeing him helpless in a hospital bed planted in me a compulsion to do whatever I thought I needed to as soon as possible, because death might be just around the corner. I also write to leave something in the world, to convince myself that I won't completely disappear when I die. I write books because I'm broken, and in some sense I'm trying to mend myself.

But the mending is shoddy, because—contrary to popular assumption—we aren't ourselves in isolation or independence. Healing from brokenness happens when we open ourselves to let others in—to confess our schemes of self-preservation, our ongoing fears, to ask for healing in our fractured bones and torn ligaments.

That's why admitting to my wife that I needed

more counseling felt so good. Finally . . . I had pulled out the creaking gears of thought and feeling, setting them on a table in front of me. From my place, my perspective, I'm still broken. I need deeper healing than my self-prescribed bandages. I need . . . help. That is my place. As the horse once said, "Asking for help isn't giving up. It's refusing to give up."[1]

God, it feels so good to know where I am, and to have someone else know.

We want to be better and stronger than we really are. We want to be in a different place from where we stand, crippled and confused. But we are most ourselves when we admit where we are. We can't get anywhere if we don't really know where we are to begin with.

Grief has shaped the stone on which I stand, for better or worse. Pretending that a boulder in the sea is a concrete foundation in the countryside won't help me be or grow. Candor is the balm for restlessness.

Know your place. State your place. Confess your place. The priest-God of truth has open ears. He knows who I am. Once I confess it, he can give me the wings I long for. He can help me leave the perch. He can make me a blackbird, ready to jump into the light

---

1. Mackesy, *The Boy, the Mole, the Fox, and the Horse*.

of a dark black night. Morning is always just on the other side.

* * *

My place, my perspective, has been shaped and colored by grief. The colors are dark, set on the paper of my life wet and running: cinder-gray of absence, Bible black fear, faded yellow longing—once red. But the colors dry. And they aren't the only ones. My place is more than grief; my perspective isn't only loss.

There are other colors, painted before the hues of grief, and after them. The deep red of passion for another, matched, reciprocated, bleeding all the way through the paper fibers. The blue-green of peace when the sun caressed the willow branches like a girl brushing the hair from her eyes. The popping orange of laughter that brings tears.

So many colors. Remove just one of them, and I wouldn't be me anymore.

The beauty of being human—transient and limited—is that the colors keep coming. "Man is born to trouble, as the sparks fly upward" (Job 5:7). But he's also born to beauty, to touch, to sound and silence. We are born to color, as the brush waves westward.

*   *   *

Annie Dillard wrote, "Beauty and grace are performed whether or not we will or sense them. The least we can do is try to be there."[2] In many ways, my father embodied beauty and grace, and my perspective, my place, was simply to try to be there—splitting and stacking wood on the driveway, noticing how the splinters and wet bark buried themselves in our gloves; marking and cutting drywall with chalked hands as our knees did the hard work; wiping away the drops of white paint before they dried, especially in those reclusive corners; resting my hand on his shoulder as he worked through a seizure; listening to his Godwords in the dark high school auditorium with the blue upholstered seats, wondering where the message and its mystery would go inside me. To try to be there for his beauty and grace—that's all.

But I think Annie Dillard would agree that beauty and grace—as divine birds soaring in and out of God's

---

2. Annie Dillard, *Pilgrim at Tinker Creek* (New York: Harper Perennial Modern Classics, 2013), 10.

great barn—do much of their work without us. We try to be there, but we miss most of it. It's a gift to notice anything at all.

And that means my perspective, my place, is shepherded. God is always extending his long wooden crook to nudge my woolen shoulders. What I saw in my father throughout my childhood has less to do with my trying and more to do with God's giving: that unexplainable "just showing up" for ordinary moments that etched themselves on my memory. I can't claim responsibility for seeing what I've seen; I try so little. Someone greater than I am wanted me to see what I've seen, to carry the memories, to paint them in this book and scatter them around the corners of my consciousness. Someone greater.

Perspective, we say, is what you make it. There's some truth to that. We can try to be intentional, to witness the beauty and grace in our blood. But when we pause, when a forest full of white-clad winter trees draws our gaze and reminds us of how much beauty and grace are swirling around us, deep and potent and chilling as the snow, we say, "My God... what have I been missing?"

In his book *The Denial of Death*, Ernest Becker recounts a tradition in psychology that suggests people can only take so much of life—even the good parts—and so they sabotage themselves in moments of wild thrill and ecstasy. It's too much. They have to pull themselves away. But maybe what's really going on is that life, mingled with death and foreshadows of resurrection and rebirth, is so swelled with beauty and grace—with meaning and gifts—that our cup overflows, as king David's did (Ps. 23:5). And we don't know what to do with an overflowing cup. Maybe that cup, with its contents pouring over the arched edge, is meant to draw our eyes up to see who is holding the pitcher. And even if we can't see anyone there (we never do), we can still speak, "Thank you," and then run after our words like a child bolting into an open field.

* * *

Who am I? What makes me a human? I am transient. I am limited. I have a place, and I have *hope*.

Hope

Hope is the most bizarre of our behaviors, but it's also the most human. Passing away as we are, limited as we are, standing in our own place, what else could we do but hope? Hope is simply realizing our limitations and yet yearning for more, believing in more, beyond anything we can see or calculate.

"Now hope that is seen is not hope. For who hopes for what he sees? But if we hope for what we do not see, we wait for it with patience" (Rom. 8:24–25).

I am waiting. I have been waiting for my dad since the moment I watched him die . . . waiting with grief, with frustration, with longing, with gratitude. Always waiting.

I've always thought of this in a negative light. Waiting is something we do with absence, when our hands are empty and our fingers begging to bend around something again.

But I have been wrong. Waiting is the recognition that something else must come. Hope is the boldness of believing that it will.

*   *   *

We all travel through transience. We lift our arms and legs in a land of limitation. And in that travel and movement, we find our place, seeing the present from our past. But all of this is leading to something. "We rejoice in our sufferings, knowing that suffering produces endurance, and endurance produces character, and character produces hope . . ." (Rom. 5:3–4).

Hope. It can strike us like starlight in a black sky. But if often comes on the coattails of character.

Character—that mysterious pool of mental traits and habits distinguishing us, identifying us—is crafted.

I used to work with soap stone in college. Chiseling away at the soft, green-gray rock would leave my hands covered in silk dust. From a mass would come a shape, one shaving at a time. From a shape would come a form. Then, when the form was right, refining began, cutting away corners and little shoulders of rock. Then multiple phases of sanding, rubbing away smaller and smaller bits of dust. The sanding was done with water, and the finer grains of sandpaper blessed the stone with a beautiful patina—as if, the whole time, there was a voice hidden in the rock that finally could sing to your eyes.

The final work, the distinguished piece, would house every hammer swing and sandpaper rubbing in its history. The present would stand in front of a hard-fought past. That's character. Character is not just the way we are; it is the way we have been.

And God says that character makes something. What does it make? What have all my years of mourning and longing for my father made? Hope.

It's hard to see the relation, isn't it? Character strives towards light. It gazes up and beyond. The Apostle Paul rejoiced in something. What? "In hope of the glory of God" (Rom. 5:2). Hope in divine light, in a self-giving aura that would somehow embrace, guide, and shelter his soul.

Character makes hope because it's always pulling us towards hope. Character is the water. Hope is the sun. Evaporation is ongoing.

* * *

Even now, it sounds ridiculous to say that all loss, every instant of longing for my father, every fear of death, every memory made bitter by his absence, was tethered to hope. But that's because I cut so much out of the journey.

Even Paul said that the path to hope goes through three countries with tough terrain: suffering, endurance, and character. The haven of hope comes only after pain, waiting, and a thousand choices. It's a long way. But that's how grief works on us, too. Nothing can be rushed or forced. The process is slow, spread over years—which is the very thing that makes us ignorant of the process. Connecting A, B, and C is far easier to notice in a day than a decade. The process gets lost on us. We claim to be wanderers, nomads in a great plain of grief. Where are we going? When did we set out? Wasn't it just last week that I noticed how thick my dad's fingers were and how his gold wedding band hugged the skin of his ring finger? Was it so long ago that I batted a whiffle ball into the high branches of the red oak tree—to the amazement of my father and myself?

Time has a way of making us feel like dazed nomads. "Didn't we just . . ?" "Where are we going?" "Oh, now I remember."

I've felt lost many times, wandering in circles through the tall grass of suffering, sitting on the stone of endurance, hammering through a wall of character. We do so much. Can we remember where we've been, who we've become, what light is calling us ahead?

* * *

Hope follows character, but it's also a mark of our humanity—to yearn for what we cannot see, for what can't be seen. It looks like madness, and many try to explain it away—as if it were a child's old crayon drawing that must, in the end, be gotten rid of. We can't afford to keep everything. But the moment we drop it in the wastebasket, we know: We've given up gold.

* * *

The beauty of hope is in its defiance. Everything can mount against it—experience, reason, physicality—and still it stands like a rooted tree in an open field, quiet but determined, ready to weather a hurricane of doubt.

* * *

Part of my hope was born the very night I watched my father die. After he took his final breath, I could actually feel one soul being subtracted from the room. There were nine people. And then there were eight. That was a piercing light of clarity amidst the pain and confusion: More is going on than can be seen.

* * *

I hope for things right now, just as you do. What is it that calls us to be defiant of the bleakness, to stand up in a world full of moments that push us down? To feel nine minus eight and wonder?

* * *

Hope seems to find us; it comes from the outside and simply whispers, "More." More than we can see, than we can understand, than we should reasonably deduce from our circumstances. More.

Hope is what made my dying father point up at the blue expanse and say, "Home." We may have reasons to hope, but ultimately hope surpasses explanation. It defies despair. It leans into the darkest places. Anyone who calls hope a childish thing is right; it is childish because children are brilliantly defiant of our block-building, our harsh reasoning. Defiance is a good thing if the adversary is dark. My best moments are when I'm most childlike, when belief gathers itself together inside me and says, "No matter what."

God recognizes this. He has a kingdom, you know. And he said, "Whoever does not receive the kingdom of God like a child will never enter it" (Mark 10:15). To see great things, you must become small. To have hope, you must be defiant enough to stand before mountains and skyscrapers, the tiny among the tall, and say, "Size doesn't matter. I'm staying here. Something good will come."

* * *

Hope makes us human because it threads together the other elements: transience, limitation, and perception.

At this very moment, I'm withering like a blade of grass—the color is leaving me. I'm melting from green to gold, readying my soul for the wind. I am my transient self. And yet in the midst of that transience, even as my mind swells with memories of my father's death, I hope for an existence that doesn't wither, an evergreen existence. Why? Where does that hope come from? Someone else, someone beyond me, someone Andrew Peterson refers to his Wingfeather Saga as "the Maker." Hope comes from a country and kingdom beyond time. It finds us in hospital rooms, at the bedside of our dying parent. It meets us, our transient selves, with a plain invitation inscribed with red crayon: "More." More than transience, more than chlorophyll fading, more than bones fracturing and shallow breathing, more than morphine dripped through clenched teeth, more than a cemetery, more than obituaries can carry, more than eyesight blurring and memory fading like floral, more. Hope calls us beyond transience.

Hope also calls to us in our limitation. We build our worlds out of can'ts. I can't lift this chair. I can't understand God. I can't delay death. Many of these can'ts turn positive because they open us up to relationships. They show us who we are, not who we want to be. And yet we know limitation in itself is not an evil. I can't be my own mother. I can't control my children. I can't write checks to solve everyone else's problems. But my limitations make a way for others. They allow space and freedom and joy and passion.

The good things that limitation allows—I hope for them. I hope through them. I hope into a place where limitation always leads to love. I hope in the redemption of all that limitation seems to steal—especially life itself. My hope is tied to my transience and also to my limitation.

And hope is also tethered to my perception. I hope from here, from where I stand, from my place. I hope as the boy who dropped his red pocket knife in the woods and never found it. I hope as the kid who made an ignorant joke about a woman with cancer outside a diner, and who then closed his mouth in shame for a long time. I hope as the teenager who got lost in the library reading Hamlet. I hope as that same teenager waiting patiently for each of my dad's seizures to end, staying as still as stones while the rest of the world careened on.

I hope as the new father whose heart sank as the nurses did a routine heel prick on his first-born. (Why couldn't they leave his blood alone?) I hope as the man who daily stares at his wife and marvels at how God made her and how she could possibly see beauty inside him. I hope as I tell her and my kids, "My father would have loved you." I hope now as the man pinning his thoughts to paper, waiting to see where each sentence will take him. I hope as myself.

*   *   *

I've carried hope with me since the day I was born, lodging it in a blue jean pocket where no one could see. It is a hope for more. More than the rising sun yawning behind the sleeping black trees. More than the giant arms of my father, circling my body for one last embrace. More than the laughter and joy I release each day in my cheek muscles and unmeasured breaths.

I hope for a face, for the eyes of a God no one can capture. I hope for the face of God. As I write that down on paper, I sense how abstract it sounds, how oddly impersonal. But we don't hope for what we see around us. We think we do, but that's a counterfeit of hope. "Hope that is seen is not hope, for who hopes for what he sees?" (Rom. 8:24). The counterfeit . . . is time. All that we see is all that has happened to us. We hope for eternity. It's that which makes us human. To be transient and limited and set in one place, to be fading like a photograph left in the sun, all the while begging to get beyond photography, to find the one with the camera. To have ignorance, weakness, and the hard door of death limit us and yet long for some deep communion with the one who can shelter us in our limitation. To see the world from our memory-drenched patch of soil and long for the gardener—this is hope. We're always confusing time with eternity. Hope reaches for what's beyond time, what's outside of it. If we hope for something we can see, that's not really hope; that's longing. There's a family resemblance between the two, but hope is the noble elder brother you're always looking up to. Longing has its places and purposes, but hope chases after the more.

I don't just long for my father. I hope for him; I hope because of him. Because his lungs stopped heaving air, because he stepped off the path of the living and into the wild woods of eternity, I hope. I hope for what I can't see. My dad's death taught me that much. In a transient, limited, place-bound existence, who would hope for what he can see?

* * *

I have my memories. I have my moments. These are not enough to hope in. There must be more.

The Song of Being Human

Patrick Park wrote a song that's always stuck with me—one line in particular: "Maybe life is a song but you're scared to sing along / until the very ending."

My father's death seemed to carry me to the very ending. Being a human is a lot like standing in a room with a song floating through the air. We're scared—of transience, of limitation, of simply being where we are. But there is a hope that one day we might break into the melody, join the path of the music, sing along by accepting who we are.

I still fight it. I want another song, or just a free pass to sit against the wall like a kid tired of gym class. But I have my moments when I dare to sing ... maybe even a few when I open my mouth and let out some unvoiced syllables.

God, I want to sing. Give me the courage to stop being mute.

*   *   *

Wherever you are, you're in it—the song of humanity. You're passing away right now. Can you feel it? The bark on the trees outside is aging. The heartwood tires of its yearly ring-building. The pith is older than it was yesterday. The trees still sway, but ever so differently from the way they did an hour ago, a minute ago, a moment ago. We don't even see it. But transience is all around us, and in our bodies and minds. Life is floral. We are floral. Flowers don't weep at being a sprout, or a stem, or a glorious crown, or a skeleton falling to support the courageous grass around them.

I know my transience. But I don't sing that part of life's song too loudly. I let others sing it. I let my dad sing it from his hospital bed. And I just listened. I let my grandmother sing it from her apartment couch, where she knit a brittle blanket to hold off the Leukemia. I let others sing it. But at least I know the words now. It's taken years to learn them, and we can't do much to rush the learning. Eventually, we just find our lips opening and closing to that truth, accepting it. And singing.

* * *

The song is about our limitation, too. The little limitations are mostly accepted. We sing with agitation, but we grow used to it, and then we accept it, even seeing the good in it.

But death is the limitation that jars us most. How could we not exist on this planet one day? Where did my dad go? He went where his hope was. I will go where my hope is, because death is a door, not a pit or an unending cave in the black. Doors bring entrance. They bring new beginnings. Death is not a dead-end; it's a threshold to a country where God's eyes are right in front of us. I can sing that song. I can sing about God's face. I can sing about home as I stare at the blue sky.

* * *

And I will sing from my place, though it's always changing. I will sing as myself, the only one God has ever made or will ever make. I will sing from my uniqueness. It's my dad's song, with all of his idiosyncrasies, that I still hear. He taught me that it's okay to sing mine. No one else will.

* * *

But hope is what gets the most beautiful notes in life's song. It's the pull upward, to more. It's the flock of starlings waving the flag of beauty, signaling to the Maker that they see him. It's not a flag of surrender; it's a flag of allegiance—waving violently before the gates of heaven. "We are coming! We belong with the light! See us!"

* * *

Loss is devastating. It brings us down to the dirt. But that is where plants grow. That is where we grow.

Transience. Limitation. Perspective. Hope. Our humanity is here.

Letter to Dad

Dear Dad,

I'm still here, very far from that bedside where you departed from us. Do you see me? I'm trying to gather the courage to sing the song of life each day. Most of the time I still get tossed by trivialities. But I'm trying.

I have three grandkids for you. They have seen your picture and have been told you're wild, like daddy. They are just beginning to hear and embrace the first words of life's song, and it's a joy to watch them—noticing their own voices, their fingertips, their need of laughter.

I still get lost, dad. I still have moments of panic, fear, of shameless pride. But God helps me see them for what they are. And I'm called back to the hope that goes beyond myself.

You are there, in that hope. You're still teaching me.

I wanted to let you know that I'm building a boat to get where you are, and I have named it "Hope."

It's ethereal, but strong. The pieces come from somewhere outside me. The hull is coming together now, and the mast is in the center, thick and bold. It will be a while before it's ready for the water, I think, but it will be ready in time.

I promise I will keep trying to sing. I won't wait until the very ending.

See you soon.

— Taylor

Thank You

Reading is an act of love. Thank you for reading this book. It was an honor to write for you.

The greatest compliment you can give to any writer is to tell someone else about the book. Please do that if you feel so led. You can also leave a review on Amazon, which goes a long way in showing others that these words might help them.

www.ingramcontent.com/pod-product-compliance
Lightning Source LLC
Chambersburg PA
CBHW020913080526
44589CB00011B/584